MW01519154

Terrance Talks Travel: The Quirky Tourist Guide to Lapland (Arctic Circle) & Helsinki, Finland

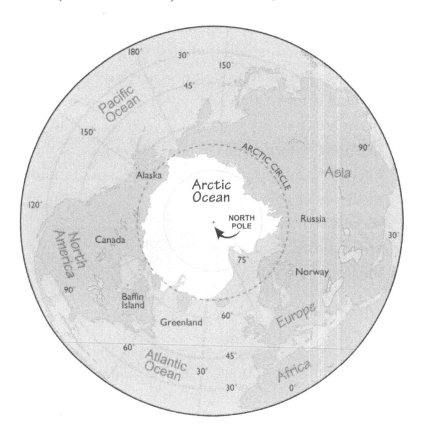

Terrance Zepke

Library of Congress Cataloging-in-Publication
Data

ISBN-10:1942738436
ISBN-13: 9781942738534

Zepke, Terrance
*Terrance Talks Travel: The Quirky Tourist Guide
to Lapland (Arctic Circle)* & Helsinki, Finland

1. Travel-Finland. 2. Adventure Travel-Polar
Regions. 3. Rovaniemi. 4. Northern Lights-Aurora
Borealis. 5. Helsinki. 6. Finland Guidebook. 7.
Northern Europe-Travel. 8. Scandinavia. 9. Arctic
Circle Guidebook. 10. Santa Claus Village. 11.
Lapland. 12. Travel-Arctic Circle. 13. Sami. 14.
Midnight Sun-Polar Night. 15. North Pole. 16.
Arctic Wildlife. 17. Finland National Parks. 18.
Nonfiction-Lapland Travel Guide. I. Title.

First edition

Safari Publishing

The Quirky Tourist Guide to Lapland (Arctic Circle) & Helsinki, Finland | Terrance Zepke

CONTENTS

INTRODUCTION

Lapland is located in the northernmost part of
Finland. This remote providence makes up one-
third of this Nordic nation. It is also part of the
Arctic Circle, and as such, is a great place for
adventure travelers.

This winter wonderland offers a myriad of
adrenaline-fueled activities, such as forest
snowshoe hiking, cross country skiing (home of
some of the best slopes and resorts in the world),
ice fishing, ice floating, snowmobiling, ice
karting, wildlife watching, off road biking on fat
bikes, ATVing, canoeing, berry picking (Finland
has some of the most exotic berries in the
world), dog sledding, reindeer sleigh rides,
photography tours, star gazing, seeing the great
Northern Lights, killer whale safaris, Lapland
Escape Room Adventure, overnight stay in a
snow igloo or ice hotel (or you can stay in a
lodge adjacent to Santa's house!), cultural tours,

moose safaris, smoke saunas, icebreaker cruises, visiting an Arctic zoo, enjoying a midnight hike and barbeque (remember that there is 24-hours of sunlight during the summer), and much more. Have you ever seen frozen waterfalls? *Amazing!* Have you ever taken a walk in the middle of a frozen ocean? *Memorable!*

Lapland is a magical place, known as the Land of the Midnight Sun, Polar Night, the Land of the Thousand Lakes, and the home of Santa Claus. It has the lowest crime rate in the world, there is no pollution, rare animals roam freely (and safely), and there is a shared belief that this land belongs to all of us. In fact, there is a law called 'Everyman's Right' whereby you have the right to live off the land, such as picking all the berries and mushrooms you like. You also have the right to ski, bike, camp, and hike freely. This means you do not need or pay any fees or obtain any permits, and it doesn't matter who owns the land. You have permission to pass through. There is a network of open wilderness wood huts that span across all the national parks of Lapland. Most have campfire set ups and are available for free for anyone to use.

I have shared all there is to see and do in this remarkable region of the world and you'll be amazed at all the possibilities! If you can imagine it, you can do it. There is no better place for an adventure traveler.

Lapland is the least densely populated place in Finland. There are more reindeer than people in this part of the world! The ratio of saunas to Finns is 1:1. The Santa Clause Village Post Office processes more than 500,000 pieces of mail annually. There are more than 750 fells or fjalls (mountains or moor-covered hills), and 188,000 lakes.

The great thing about an Arctic adventure is that all ages can enjoy it. Most activities are geared towards kids and adults, so this is a great family experience. And who doesn't want to see Santa's workshop? Or take a ride with a reindeer? Or have a chat with Santa?

I have included Helsinki as most folks fly into this city and explore it on the way to Lapland or back. However long you stay and whatever you decide to do, this will be a once-in-a-lifetime adventure.

So read on to learn how to make the most out of your time in Lapland. Be sure to pay special attention to my TOP TEN PICKS, Annual Events, and FYI boxes.

FYI: The Polar Night occurs in the northernmost and southernmost regions of the Earth when the night lasts for more than 24 hours. This occurs only inside the polar circles. The opposite phenomenon, the polar day, or Midnight Sun occurs when the sun stays above the horizon for more than 24 hours.

GETTING THERE

By Air

There are daily commercial flights from Helsinki to Rovaniemi, which is the gateway to Lapland. The flight lasts about seventy minutes and this is the cheapest air option. Or you can arrange a charter flight to Lapland. Also, there are direct flights on Finnair, Lufthansa, Germania, and Norwegian to Rovaniemi from most major European cities, such as London, Warsaw, and Berlin.

https://www.finavia.fi/en/airports/rovaniemi and
https://www.finavia.fi/en/airports/helsinki-airport

Note: There are other places you can arrive in Lapland, such as Tornio, Kemi, and Levi, but logistically it makes the most sense to arrive into Rovaniemi.

 By Train

This is a great option for those wanting to see more of the countryside. The train takes about ten hours to get from Helsinki to Rovaniemi, but the time flies! There are sleeping cars if you take the night train.

https://www.vr.fi/cs/vr/en/frontpage

For a special experience…

You can choose to experience Lapland via the **Arctic Circle Train**, which is considered to be one of the greatest rail experiences in the world. You will see spectacular scenery, such as glaciers, waterfalls, huge lakes, mountains, fjords, and Nordic villages. The train includes a dozen stops between Kiruna, Sweden and Narvik, Norway, such as Abisko National Park, Ice Hotel, and Björkliden Ski Resort. To reach Kiruna, the best option is the night train from Stockholm.

http://www.scandinavianrail.com/scenicrail/sweden/arctic-circle-train and www.eurail.com/pass.

Additionally, you participate in a longer railway adventure of sixteen days. You cross the Arctic Circle on Day 5. The trip includes hotel stays and a fjord cruise.

https://www.greatrail.com/us/tours/arctic-circle-express/

 By Car

You can drive from Helsinki to Rovaniemi or if you take the train, they can accommodate your vehicle so you will have it upon arrival. If you drive you will most likely take Highway E75. Along the way you will pass through some scenic villages, quaint towns, and see many natural wonders. Another option is to rent a car upon arrival in Rovaniemi.

 By Bus

There are a couple of bus companies that will take you from Helsinki to Rovaniemi. The trip is longer but scenic and affordable. Matkahuolto (https://matkahuolto.fi/en/) and Onnibus (https://www.onnibus.com/home)

By Cruise

If you want to experience an Arctic icebreaker cruise, you will depart from Kemi. These day cruises will be discussed later in this reference. Additionally, there are Arctic Circle cruises that last a week or more.

Getting Around Rovaniemi

Most tour companies will pick you at your accommodations (and return you there afterwards) for activities you have booked with them. The public bus service in Rovaniemi is good. Timetables, routes and ticket prices can be found on www.linkkari.fi. There is a bus that goes directly to Santa Claus Village and the Arctic Treehouse Hotel (seasonally). Matkahuolto operates daily coach service to Ranua Zoo. https://www.matkahuolto.fi/en/.

Additionally, there is taxi service and a shuttle service to and from the airport.

Fast Facts

Country Size: Finland is 130,558 square miles. Lapland is 38,752 square miles and Rovaniemi is 3,095 square miles.

Capital: Helsinki

Median age: 40

Population: 61,763 in Rovaniemi, 179,997 in Lapland, 642,045 in Helsinki, and 5.5 million in Finland.

Currency: Euro

Official Language: Finnish is most commonly spoke but also Swedish and English too.

Time Zone: Eastern European Time (UTC+02:00 time zone, 2 hours ahead of Coordinated Universal Time. The zone uses daylight saving time, so that it uses UTC+03:00 during the summer).

Voltage: 230V and frequency 50 Hz.

Nickname: Land of a Thousand Lakes

Leading Export: Finland's biggest exports are machinery, mineral fuels, and iron & steel.

The providence of Lapland is divided into sixteen municipalities (Simo, Keminmaa, Ylitornio, Pello, Kolari, Muonio, Enontekiö, Kittilä, Ranua, Posi, Salla, Pelkosenniemi, Savukoski, Sodankylä, Inari, and Utsjoki) and four cities (Kemi, Kemijärvi, Tornio, and Rovaniemi).

Flag of Finland

Documentation: All tourists except those from Scandinavian countries are required to have a passport to enter the country. Visas are not required for most tourists, but citizens of some countries will have to apply for a visa to visit Finland. U.S. citizens may enter Finland for up to

90 days for tourist or business purposes without a visa. Your passport should be valid for at least six months beyond the period of stay. No vaccinations are required. You cannot enter or exit the country with more than 10,000 euros. EU citizens do not need a passport or visa. https://www.worldtravelguide.net/guides/europe/finland/passport-visa/

Currency Exchange: The only money exchange options in Rovaniemi are banks. Their hours are short so be sure to plan accordingly. You can also use an exchange bureau at the Helsinki Airport. Visa® and MasterCard® are widely accepted. Please note that there are some shops in Santa's Village that only accept cash. www.oanda.com.

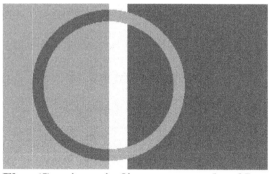

Sami Flag (Sami are indigenous people of Lapland)

FYI: There are no internet cafés in Rovaniemi, but many places offer free Wi-Fi for customers. You can also buy a prepaid mobile data connection from kiosks. Public computers are available at Rovaniemi Tourist Information and the City Library.

Best Time to Visit: It depends on what you want to do. If you want to see the Northern Lights, enjoy certain activities like snowmobiling, or participate in Christmas celebrations, you will need to go in the winter. I think the best time to go is in the winter. It is peak tourist season, so prices will be higher. However, if you want to go hiking, canoeing, horseback riding, enjoy riverboat cruises, or exploring national parks or islands such as Inari, it is best to go during the summer.

Of course, it gets quite cold in the winter with temperatures often dropping well below zero. I will discuss more about the weather and what to expect later in this reference.

Nov-March is the winter season with a lot of snow and darkness. There is only a few hours of daylight during the winter. However, December is still a magical time to visit. January and February are considered to be Midwinter. The best months to see the Northern Lights are September – March with peak months being December-February. The best time is between 9 p.m. – 1 a.m.

Spring arrives in May and is lovely but only lasts a few weeks.

The summer season is mid-June to mid-August with July being the warmest month. The average temperatures will be 60-70°F. This is the time of the Midnight Sun when there is more than twelve hours of sunlight a day. This is the time to visit if you wish to canoe, hike, fish, raft, or enjoy other summer activities. Santa Village is open year round.

***Warning!* Lapland is notorious for mosquitoes during the summer, so bring good insect repellent and wear long sleeves and pants. There is an abundance (and I mean A LOT!) of these pesky creatures because of the many lakes, swamps, and forests.**

Autumn is as short as spring in Lapland, lasting from mid-August to mid-September. Snow usually arrives by October.

TERRANCE'S TOP TEN PICKS

1. **Try a sauna.** Saunas are to Finland what
   pubs are to England. They are everywhere
   and there are all kinds and they are quite
   popular with locals and tourists alike. Most
   hotels have saunas, but I recommend
   Kesarafla Sauna in Rovaniemi. Located on

the Kemijoki River, it features a lovely terrace restaurant. Open during the summer. https://www.visitrovaniemi.fi/eat-and-drink/kesarafla-sauna/. Or try a <u>Sauna Gondola</u>. This sauna is situated on a ski lift. Yes, a ski lift! Up to four people may enjoy this mile high twenty-minute sauna. http://www.yllas.fi/en/services/sauna-gondola.html. Another unique experience is the <u>Sauna Raft</u>. You are taken on a raft onto the Kemijoki River where you will enjoy a sauna aboard a floating raft, *M/S Erkin Arkki*. Afterwards, you may take a dip in the refreshing river. https://www.saunalauttarovaniemi.com/4. If you're looking for luxurious, look no farther than the <u>Arctic Forest Spa</u>, which also includes Jacuzzis, champagne, and lots of sauna options.

https://santaparkarcticworld.com/arctic-forest-spa. Or try an authentic smoke sauna (The Finnish people swear by this). Wood is burned in a big stove and smoke fills the room (no chimney). When the sauna is hot enough, the fire is allowed to die and the smoke is ventilated out. The residual heat of the stove is enough for the duration of the sauna. This creates a gentle heat that perfectly soothes achy muscles and joints. https://www.kiilopaa.fi/en/outdoor-activities/smoke-sauna.html.

FYI: There are roughly five million people and three million saunas in Finland, which averages out to one per household. At one time, Finnish mothers gave birth in saunas.

2. **See the Aurora Borealis.** Also known as the Northern Lights, this is a natural electrical phenomenon characterized by the appearance of reddish or greenish streaks of light, usually near the northern or southern magnetic pole. It is best to use a tour company for your best chance to see these strange and wonderful lights, such as Aurora Service Tours, http://tours.aurora-service.eu/ or Tromso Safaris for photography enthusiasts, https://tromsosafari.no/.

We had a cookout (roasted sausages and cocoa) while on our Northern Lights adventure. The fire and good food helped keep us warm on a very cold night. We saw the Aurora Borealis so it was well worth it, but it was COLD! Our outing was supposed to be for three hours but our guide liked us (?) and kept us out for five hours. That's me hugging the fire. Did I mention it was cold?

3. One of our most thrilling experiences in the Arctic was a **Husky Safari**. Everyone gets their own team and you set out on your expedition after getting a briefing and a chance to meet your canine safari guides for the day. Despite what they tell you, the huskies only know '*Go!*' They do not slow down or stop, trust me. And they are incredibly fast! Our team went so fast that we got dumped out rounding a turn halfway into our outing. Within minutes, a guide arrived on a snowmobile and took us back to join our group and our huskies. We took turns with one of us steering the team and the other sitting in the sled. Both were crazy fun! You are given snowsuits to wear for the day and we were never cold or uncomfortable. After

our expedition, we enjoyed hot chocolate

while shedding our snowsuits.

https://huskypark.fi/en/

**Here we are on a short rest break. That's me and my
team.**

4. **Visit Santa**. You absolutely MUST visit Santa Claus Village. Rovaniemi is Santa's hometown. He has set up a wonderful workshop, restaurants, lodges, post office, shops, and more. You can have your photo taken with Santa if you like, but there is a fee. During this outing, you can check off several adventures, including snowmobiling, a reindeer sleigh ride (the reindeer ride is suitable for all ages as the reindeer move rather slowly and you are inside a padded sleigh), and a chat with Santa. Be sure to stop for an Arctic Circle photo opp. One thing worth mentioning is that snowmobiling is hard work. These are big, powerful pieces of machinery and you are moving at fairly high speeds. The trade-off for your efforts is the

incredible adrenaline rush you'll experience

as you race through the snow.

https://santaclausvillage.info/

**That's me posing under the Arctic Circle
sign.**

5. Enjoy a night snowshoe hike through the forest. With only the moonlight, stars, and pure white snow to guide you, you are as close to nature as you can get. Or enjoy a full day of snowshoeing in Oulanka National Park where you'll see waterfalls, frozen lakes, beautiful snow-laden pine trees, and some wildlife, if you're lucky. This is a chance to truly connect with nature that is hard to find except in the Arctic where the population is smaller than land mass. Or you can go skiing or snowboarding if you are looking for more thrills. The park is also a great place during the summer season with boat rides, canoeing, and trail hiking.
https://www.laplandsafaris.com/en/activities/skiing-snow-shoes

6. **Stay in a hotel made entirely of ice!** The
   Arctic Snow Hotel has been reinventing itself
   every year since 2008. The hotel opens mid-
   December and stays open until the ice starts
   to melt in late March. There are thirty guest
   (ice) rooms, an ice chapel, ice restaurant, and
   ice bar, which is where guests spend a great
   deal of time! The temperature stays 30 -
   40°F. There are all kinds of rooms available,
   including family suites. The beds are made of
   ice but have mattresses and reindeer hides on

top. Fair warning! This is still a cold experience as you are in an ice room laying on a block of ice! But it is a unique experience and fairly fun if you spend some time in the bar before bedtime. They also have snow igloos if an ice room scares you. Also, the main building has an open fireplace and hot drinks are served. A good, hot breakfast is served every morning. http://arcticsnowhotel.fi/snowhotel/rooms/

Hotel Lounge & Sleep Igloos

7. **Arctic Survival Adventure**. During this
   four-hour excursion you will be taken into
   the forest and taught how to forage for food,
   fish, make a fire without matches, build an
   emergency shelter, and more. This is fun for
   the whole family or you can amp up the
   experience with an overnight stay (no
   electricity or running water).

http://www.discoveringfinland.com/destination/arctic-survival-rovaniemi/

8. **Do something extremely icy.** The Arctic offers the biggest array of extreme winter activities, such as icefall climbing, ice sculpting, ice karting, icebreaker cruises, ice floating, and ice fishing.

https://lapland.nordicvisitor.com/day-tours/rovaniemi/

9. **Take an icebreaker cruise**. The *Polar Explorer* sets off on an exciting three-hour cruise in the frozen Bothnian Sea. During your adventure cruise, you will get a guided tour of the icebreaker vessel, witness ice breaking, watch a short film about icebreakers, enjoy warm berry juice in the cozy saloon, walk on the

frozen sea, and take a polar plunge in a flotation survival suit. You will be presented with a Cruise & Swim Certificate as a keepsake of this once-in-a-lifetime experience.

https://www.icebreaker.fi/

10. **Take a cultural tour**. The Sámi are indigenous to Lapland. You can learn more about them by visiting Inari, which has a great museum and an outstanding cultural center, as well as many fine handicrafts shops. The village is situated on Lapland's largest lake, Inarijärvi. Lemmenjoki National Park and Kevo Nature Reserve are located nearby. The current population is less than 10,000 in Finland and an overall population of

80,000, including Norway, Sweden, and Russia. https://www.inari.fi/en/main-page.html

FYI: What are Northern Lights? The bright dancing lights of the aurora are collisions between electrically charged particles from the sun that enter the earth's atmosphere. The lights are seen above the magnetic poles of the northern and southern hemispheres. They are known as 'Aurora Borealis' in the north and 'Aurora Australis' in the south. Aurora displays appear in many colors although pale green and pink

are the most common. Shades of red, yellow, green, blue, and violet have been reported. The lights appear in many forms from patches or scattered clouds of light to streamers, arcs, rippling curtains or shooting rays that light up the sky with an eerie glow.

.

FYI: Many cultures have legends about these lights. In Roman myths, Aurora was the goddess of the dawn. In medieval times, the occurrences of Aurora were seen as harbingers of war or famine. The Maori of New Zealand shared a belief with many northern people of Europe and North America that the lights were reflections from torches or campfires. The Menominee Indians believed that the lights indicated

the location of manabai'wok (giants) who were the spirits of great hunters and fishermen. The Alaskan Inuit believed that the lights were the spirits of the animals they hunted. The Aboriginal believed that the lights were the spirits of their people.

Get in the mindset for your trip by making some classic Nordic cuisine. Here are two traditional recipes.

Finnish Meatballs – Lihapullat (a very common Finnish dish)

- 1 lb. ground beef (or you can use half beef and half ground pork)
- 1/2 cup dry breadcrumbs. breadcrumbs

- 3.4 cup kermaviili" (substitute cream, milk, yogurt or crème fraiche)
- 1 egg
- 2 chopped onions
- 1/2 tsp salt
- 1/2 tsp allspice
- 1/4 tsp white pepper
- 1/2 tsp paprika

Heat the oven to 425 °F

In a large bowl soak the breadcrumbs in the kermaviili (or in the liquid of your choice), leave for 10-15 minutes. It should appear moist but not hard or runny. Adjust the amount, if using a substitution, according to the softness of the mixture so that it is the correct consistency.

Fry the onions in butter in a skillet until soft, set aside to cool.

Add the egg, mince, onions and seasonings to the breadcrumb mix.

Knead the mixture thoroughly until well combined and firm. Shape into whatever sized balls you prefer (I like them small) with slightly oiled or moist hands (keep a bowl with water nearby) and place them on a greased shallow baking tray. Bake for 20 minutes or until golden.

While the meatballs are baking, you can make the gravy.

Gravy – Ruskea kastikke ("brown sauce")

- 1 -2 tbsp butter
- 2-3 tbsp flour
- 1-2 cups beef stock
- salt and pepper to taste

Boil the stock and keep it warm. Melt the butter in a large skillet and add the flour, mixing until the "paste" turns golden brown. Start pouring the hot stock using a whisk to constantly mix it in. Stir well so that there are no lumps. Season with salt and pepper to taste.

Serve with potatoes and lingonberry jam.

Yum!

JOULUTORTTU – FINNISH CHRISTMAS JAM TARTS

Pastry:
2 cups unsalted butter; cubed, at room temperature
2 cups light ricotta
4 cups of plain flour
Mix butter and flour together with fingers to form a crumby consistency. Add ricotta and mix until it all comes together to form dough. Roll into a ball then flatten into a disc shape and cover and refrigerate for about half an hour.

Filling:
10-12 oz. pitted prunes
4 tbsp sugar
Water – just enough to cover the prunes in a medium sized saucepan

Jam:
Soak prunes for 2 hours, rinse, and place into a saucepan.
Add water and sugar to the pan. Bring to the boil then
reduce heat and simmer until the prunes have completely
softened (about 15-20 minutes). Stir often so they do not
stick to the pan. Once the prunes are soft and most of the
water has been absorbed, remove from the heat. If you
want a smooth texture you can puree the jam or just mash
with a fork.

Divide pastry dough into three piles. Roll out the first pile,
fold into three (like an envelope) and roll out again into a
square shape about 1/2" thick. Use flour sparingly so the
pastry dough does not stick to the board. Cut the pastry
into squares. Make diagonal cuts in each corner of every
square about halfway to the center leaving the middle of
the square uncut for the jam. Place a teaspoon of jam into
the center of each square.

To make a windmill shape, lift one corner of a square and
fold into the middle on top of the jam. Brush the top of the
pastry corner with lightly beaten egg, and fold the next
corner on top of the egg. Continue with the last 2 corners.
Press firmly in the middle to ensure the corners stick. Place
the pastries onto a baking tray and brush all over with
lightly beaten egg. Bake at 425°F for ten minutes or until
golden brown and slightly puffed.

Dust with icing sugar when cool. Instead of prunes, you
can use any jam you like, such as apricot or strawberry.

Makes approx. 60 pieces. If you want to make a smaller quantity simply halve the recipe.

FYI: Cloudberry is the world's most expensive berry. It grows in Finnish swamps. It is red until it ripens and turns orange. It is loaded with Vitamin C. It is commonly sold in shops as cloudberry jam. In addition to cultivated berries, there are roughly fifty species of wild berries that grow in Finland with three dozen of these being edible. The most commonly eaten berries include lingonberries, bilberries, cloudberries, raspberries, cranberries, wild strawberries, bog whortleberries, mountain crowberries, sea-buckthorn berries, and rowanberries.

Popular Finnish Lapland Dishes

KARJALANPIIRAKKA (Karelian pies) are hand-sized pies filled with potatoes, rice or carrots.

KALAKUKKO are larger than Karjalanpiirakka and are filled with fish instead of vegetables. They are most commonly filled with muikku, a small herring-like fish found in the Lake District of Eastern Finland.

GRILLIMAKKARA are big sausages eaten with mustard

RUISLEIPÄ (rye bread) is made from sour dough and is a staple of the Finnish diet.

NÄKKILEIPÄ is the cracker version of rye bread and there are also many kinds, including the Finn Crisp cracker. They are eaten at breakfast with butter, cheese and other spreads, with soups at lunch, or as an evening snack.

KORVAPUUSTI translates into "slapped ears" (similar to American cinnamon buns)

SILLI JA UUDET PERUNAT are new
potatoes with herring (silli) or fish roe. New
potatoes with fresh lake fish and chanterelle
sauce.

RAPU are small fresh water lobsters are
considered a gourmet treat and are only
available seasonally.

PORONKÄRISTYS is a popular dish made
with reindeer meat, which is one of the
healthiest foods you can eat as it is pure, lean
protein and high in B-12, omega-3, an omega-6.
This dish is typically served with mashed
potatoes.

LEIPÄJUUSTO ("Finnish Squeaky Cheese"
and also called Juustoleipä or "cheese bread"),
this mild cheese is most often made from cow's
milk but can also be made from reindeer or
goat's milk. The milk is first curdled and then
fried or baked in a pie tin and cut in wedges. It is
often served with cloudberry jam.

More Finnish Favorites: Kaalikääryleet are cabbage rolls filled with beef, onions, and spices and served with a side of lingonberry jam to give it just the right amount of sweet and salty. These stuffed rolls are delicious! Seriously, you have to try them. Also, Lohikeitto (salmon soup), Mustikkapiirakka (blueberry pie), and Vispipuuro (whipped lingonberry porridge; pictured here), which is another one of my favorites. The Finns favorite candy is Salmiakki (salty liquorice) and Fazer Blue chocolate.

Vispipuuro

TOURISTY THINGS TO SEE & DO

Arktikum Science Center & Museum is an
excellent place to learn all about Lapland and it
is also a science center. My favorite exhibits are
Arctic in Change and Northern Ways.
http://www.arktikum.fi/en

iseum of Lapland shares the mportance of forestry in Lapland. The museum is set up in a series of lumberjacks' cabins and includes logging equipment and the first steam locomotive ever used for logging in Finland. http://www.lapinmuseot.fi/eng/rovaniemi/lapinm etsamuseo.html

Pallas-Yllästunturi National Park is the oldest national park in Finland and is the third largest park in the country. It offers many activities, according to the season: skiing, snowshoe walking, mountain biking, geocaching, fishing, berry and mushroom picking, canoeing, swimming, hiking (17 nature trails), and bird-watching, including the golden plover and long-tailed skua. http://www.nationalparks.fi/pallas-yllastunturinp/activities

Other noteworthy parks include Urho Kekkonen National Park, Oulanka National Park, Pyhä-Luosto National Park, Lemmenjoki National Park, and Perämeri National Park. Additionally, there are two nature reserves: Malla and Kevo.

FYI: There is a lot of wildlife in the Arctic, including moose, reindeer, wolves, brown bears, wolverines, killer whales, Ringed Seals, Siberian Musk Deer, Dhole, Lynx, polar bears, Arctic Foxes, Palla's Cat, and many species of birds, including Eagle Owls and the Honey Buzzard.

Ranua Zoo is a cool arctic zoo featuring fifty different species of animals indigenous to the Arctic, including polar bears and Arctic Foxes. The zoo has been designed to replicate a real

setting for the animals so it does not feel like
you are visiting a zoo.

https://english.ranuazoo.com/

Rovaniemi Art Museum is also a cultural
center that is housed in an old bus depot. This is
one of the few buildings that survived WWII. It
houses a large art collection and library of art

books. http://www.korundi.fi/en/Rovaniemi-Art-Museum/

Rovaniemi Local History Museum is a collection of open-air museums designed to be a living history for visitors. The main building was a farm that survived WWII and there are log cabins containing exhibits and artifacts of Rovaniemi. The historic photos are very interesting. If you're there at Christmas, be sure to participate in their traditional porridge feast. http://www.lapinmuseot.fi/eng/rovaniemi/rovaniemenkotiseutumuseo.html

Santa's House of Snowmobiles is a small but cool little museum housed in Santa Claus Village. Snowmobiles are major forms of transportation in Lapland. This museum offers a glimpse into the history of these machines, including a 1960 Harley Davidson snowmobile (very rare!).

http://www.houseofsnowmobiles.fi/en

Santa Claus Village is the #1 attraction in Rovaniemi. The village has everything that Santa, his elves, and tourists need, including restaurants, shops, hotels, reindeer rides, and more. There is a museum chronicling the history and heritage of Christmas. Photos can be taken with Santa for a fee. Be sure to visit the post office and send a postcard to someone from Santa's Village. Tickets can be bought on site or online at

https://santaparkarcticworld.com/santapark and

more information can be found at

https://www.santaclausvillage.info/santa-claus/christmas-house-santa-exhibition/

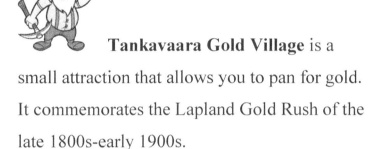

Tankavaara Gold Village is a small attraction that allows you to pan for gold. It commemorates the Lapland Gold Rush of the late 1800s-early 1900s.

http://www.tankavaara.fi/en/

Tornio Golf is the only course in the world where you can hit the ball over the international border from one country to another. You play seven holes in Finland and eleven holes in Sweden. You are literally playing in different countries and time zones!

http://torniogolf.fi/?lang=en

There are few places outside of Rovaniemi that may be of interest to you: **Kemi** (known for having the world's largest snow castle and icebreaker cruises depart from here); **Saariselkä Sport Resort** offers superb skiing and snowboarding; **Levi** has a winter sports resort that is big with the younger crowd; **Suomu** is one of the best ski resorts in Europe; **Ylläs** is another popular ski resort; **Luosto** is a home to Europe's only open amethyst mine.

FYI: More than 500,000 tourists visit Rovaniemi every year. It is a fairly even split among Finnish guests and foreign guests. Most foreigners come from Germany, France, Russia, U.K. and Israel.

Rovaniemi Church

Adventure Tours

Just about any activity and tour is possible seasonally: hiking, fishing, snowshoeing, photography tours, horseback riding, berry and mushroom picking, ice climbing, ice breaker cruises, hiking, safaris, snowmobiling, ATVing, off road biking, whale watching, fishing, culture tours, paragliding, rafting, skiing, canoeing, and dog sledding. Most tours can be arranged upon arrival in Rovaniemi, except it is best to book in advance from Christmas – New Years. Also, the most popular tours should be pre-arranged. These include husky safaris and Northern Lights tours. The Rovaniemi Tourist Information on Lordi's Square can help you book excursions. I have included a few favorites here but you can find a comprehensive list at https://www.visitfinland.com/:

Ice Fishing (You will snowmobile to perfect place to drill the hole and go fishing. You will enjoy a snow bonfire and a tasty meal of fish soup, smoked salmon, and Lapland bread).

https://www.viator.com/tours/Rovaniemi/Snow
mobile-and-Ice-Fishing-Experience/d22130-
65490P59

Icebreaker Cruise includes the Arctic cruise,
polar plunge, lunch, and glimpse at the world's
largest snow castle. www.visitkemi.fi

Ice Floating. During this three-hour adventure,
you will float among icebergs in a frozen lake in
the middle of the Finnish wilderness. The dry
suit will keep you comfortable as you watch for
the Northern Lights.

https://www.viator.com/tours/Rovaniemi/Laplan
d-Northern-Lights-Aurora-Borealis-ice-floating-
in-Rovaniemi/d22130-32988P17?pub=vcps

This 8-day Arctic expedition hits all the highlights and takes you off the beaten path to the northernmost tip of Lapland. Enjoy a smoke sauna, hike scenic trails, stay at Saariselka resort, eat delicious, local food at Laanila Kievari, visit Inari (Sami village), dig for gold, take a boat ride on River Lemmenjoki, and more.

https://julkaisut.metsa.fi/assets/pdf/lp/Esitteet/arctic-lapland-touring-route.pdf

Night Snowshoe Hike. Participants are transported to the Wilderness Lodge, which is a lovely lumberjack manor situated on the Raudanjoki River. In addition to taking a scenic snowshoe stroll, you may see the Northern Lights and you will enjoy a cookout over an open fire.

https://www.getyourguide.com/rovaniemi-
12653/rovaniemi-evening-snowshoe-hike-
t54459/

Northern Lights Snowmobiling Safari begins
with a snowmobile ride into the forests of
Lapland. You will enjoy a cookout and warm
fire and should also see the Northern Lights if all
goes well.

https://www.getyourguide.com/rovaniemi-
12653/rovaniemi-snowmobile-safari-search-for-
northern-lights-t36999/

Ranua Arctic Zoo Adventure. This is a great
outing for all ages. The forest zoo is well
designed to be optimal for the animals and
visitors, who will see 200 Arctic animals, such
as polar bears and lynxes. A buffet lunch will be

served and a stop at a Fazer candy factory will complete the day.

https://www.getyourguide.com/rovaniemi-12653/rovaniemi-day-at-ranua-wildlife-park-arctic-zoo-t94173/

Santa's Village and Snowmobile to Reindeer Farm with lunch and chat with Santa. Adventure includes a reindeer sleigh ride and a special "Crossing the Arctic Circle" ceremony.

https://www.getyourguide.com/rovaniemi-12653/visit-to-santa-s-village-and-snowmobiling-to-reindeer-farm-t94161/

Snowmobile Safari to Husky Man's Camp. This includes a couple of hours of intense snowmobiling and a visit to a husky dog camp where you will learn all about dog sledding and the importance of huskies in the Arctic. You will be served hot beverages during the storytelling and take a short sled ride.

https://www.getyourguide.com/rovaniemi-l2653/snowmobile-safari-to-the-husky-farm-from-rovaniemi-t37000/

ABOUT ACCOMMODATIONS

There is no central booking service for Rovaniemi. However, there are lots of options, ranging from budget hostels to luxury hotels. The best bet is to use www.airbnb.com or www.booking.com.

BEST LUXURY HOTEL: Arctic Light Hotel, which is housed in the former city hall, is a new and award-winning hotel. A big, wonderful breakfast is included. The restaurant offers three distinct dining areas to choose from. http://www.arcticlighthotel.fi/en/hotel/

BEST APARTMENT RENTAL: Aakenus
Apartments are located in the heart of town and
are very affordable. Aakenus apartments
includes totally 13 apartments of have different
sizes and styles. Apartment guests can use
reception, restaurant and other services of Hotel
Aakenus.

https://www.visitrovaniemi.fi/accommodation/aa
kenus-apartments/

BEST LODGE: Arctic Circle Wilderness Lodge (pictured here) is a short drive from town. Their restaurant serves good Lappish food and there is a sauna. Activities are offered by the lodge. https://wildnordic.fi/arctic-circle-wilderness-lodge/

BEST QUIRKY LODGING: **Arctic Tree House Hotel** (pictured here) offers private treehouses featuring full length glass for viewing. Each treehouse comes with its own sauna. The restaurant serves fine Finnish food. https://arctictreehousehotel.com/

BEST ARCTIC IGLOOS: **Arctic Glass Igloos**
(next door to the Arctic Snow Hotel) offers a fun
and unique way to experience the Arctic. There
are restaurants, snow saunas, ice bar, and
Jacuzzis on site.
http://arcticsnowhotel.fi/northern-lights-glass-
igloos-rovaniemi-lapland-finland/

BEST CHALET: **Christmas Chalets** are fully
decorated, cozy chalets complete with fireplaces
and Christmas trees. http://christmaschalets.com/

BEST B & B: B & B Kotitie (pictured here) is
an adorable country-style wood house just
outside of Rovaniemi so it is quiet and can
accommodate up to six. It has a bedroom,
kitchen, bathroom, and living room. Reasonable
rates. Breakfast is included and other meals can

be arranged. They offer massages and special saunas with herbal treatments and traditional Finnish vasta (birch-tree branches tied together and used to swat skin to improve circulation). Includes drinks and food. www.bb-kotitie.com.

BEST REMOTE LODGING: Hotel **Vartiosaari** is located on Aurora Island, which is ten minutes outside of Rovaniemi. The eleven-room boutique hotel boasts Finnish chic décor.

The restaurant resembles a Lappish hut.

https://www.hotelvartiosaari.fi/

BEST LUXURY LODGE: **Octola** (pictured

here) is a hybrid of log cabin, glass house, and

deluxe hotel. Located on a private island, Octola

offers private activities for its guests and features an eight-course North Pole menu in its restaurant. http://octola.com/

BEST FAMILY HOTEL: **Santasport Hotel & Kammi Hostel** offers standard and superior rooms with breakfast and swimming pool included. There is a gym and bowling alley, as well as two restaurants and a deli/lounge. Physiotherapy and massages are offered. Their best amenity is the Arctic Adventure Park Huima. http://santasport.fi/en/accommodation

BEST HOSTEL: **Hostel Café Koti** (pictured here) is new and modern in design. Choose from an apartment rental, three dorms, or two dozen different room types and styles. Breakfast is included and there is a cool roof terrace bar. https://hostelcafekoti.fi/en

BEST VILLA: **Villa Lumikko** (built in 2018) can accommodate up to ten guests. There is a big living room with fireplace and fully-equipped kitchen. There are three bedrooms and two soft beds in the living room. There is an outdoor hot tub.

https://www.visitrovaniemi.fi/accommodation/villa-lumikko/

BEST BUDGET GUESTHOUSE: **Guesthouse
Borealis** (pictured here) is at Rovaniemi Station.
En suite guest rooms come with free Wi-Fi and
parking. There are saunas and an outdoor hut for
hanging out.

http://www.guesthouseborealis.com/

FYI: There are many lodging options in Santa Claus Village, including the Nova Skyland Hotel. Staying in Santa Claus Village gives you quick access to their many options: Christmas Exhibition featuring the Elves Toy Factory, history of the Christmas tree, and most recognized Christmas traditions around the world. Plus, Santa's Office, Santa's Post Office, Elf's Farm Petting Zoo, Snowman World Winter Zone, Santa Park with Magic Train and Magical Christmas Show, shops, restaurants, coffee bar, and many activities.
https://www.visitrovaniemi.fi/accommodation/santa-claus-holiday-village/

Camping

There are several camping possibilities, but the only thing in Rovaniemi is **Ounaskoski Camping** (pictured here). As you can see, they are located on the Kemijoki River. Tents and campers are permitted. That is the Lumberjacks Bridge in the background. This location is scenic and convenient and the price is right for budget travelers. Plus, there is an on-site cafeteria. Open May-September.

https://www.visitrovaniemi.fi/accommodation/ounaskoski-camping/

RUNNER UP: Ranua Zoo Camping is open year round with tent sites and camper parking options. The sauna is always open. Amenities include a kitchen, dining area, grill, picnic area, showers and restrooms, laundry facility, children's playground, candy story, and The Wild Arctic Restaurant. Additionally, there is hiking, fishing, and canoeing nearby.

A bit about food... There are lots of good dining options in Rovaniemi, including **Restaurant Nili, Lapland Restaurant Kotahovi, Santa's Salmon Place, Reindeer Café, Paha Kurki Rockhouse, Feenix** (lunch buffet), **Café Bar 21**, and **Ravintola Roka Bistro** (vegetarian options). And, of course, there are dozens of places to eat in Santa's Village.

If you're looking for good coffee and sweets/pastries, try **Finnish Street Café, Sweet Pastries, Bakery,** or **Choco Deli. Arctic Ice Cream Factory** is a must for ice cream lovers of all ages.

If you're looking for some nightlife, **Ounasmetas Own Pub, Bar and Lounge Sfaar** (fairly new pub with entertainment), and **Comico Bar Y Restaurante** (stand-up comedy).

ABOUT LAPLAND

Exploring the Arctic

The Russians were the first to explore this region in the 11th and 12th centuries. Exploration by Europeans began in earnest in the 18th and 19th centuries. Sir Robert McClure is credited with finding the Northwest Passage in 1851. The first documented account of man reaching the North Pole is American explorer, Robert Peary, in 1909. Prior to that, only the Vikings had ventured from Scandinavia to Greenland where many settled on the southwest coast. They survived thanks to seal, sheep, and caribou.

Arctic Population

The population is about four million, including indigenous and immigrant inhabitants.

Anthropologists believe there have been people living here for more than 20,000 years, including the Inuit or Eskimos (Canada, Alaska, and Greenland), Yúpik, Iñupiat, and Athabascan (Alaska), and Sami (Finland, Norway, Sweden, and Russia). In Finland, the Sámi population is 6,000 – 9,000, and they have their own autonomous parliament of Inari, Finland.

Arctic Circle

The Arctic Circle is the parallel of latitude that runs **66° 33' 39**," or roughly 66.5°, north of the Equator. Roughly 9,000 miles to the south is the Antarctic Circle, of equal diameter to and parallel to the Arctic Circle as well as equally distant from the Equator. The Arctic Circle marks the southern extremity of the polar day of the summer solstice in June and the polar night of the winter solstice in December. Within the whole area of the Arctic Circle, the Sun is above the horizon for at least 24 continuous hours once per year, in conjunction with the Arctic's summer solstice, which is often referred to as the "midnight sun." The Arctic Ocean lies wholly within the Arctic Circle. Everything north of the Arctic Circle is properly known as the Arctic while the zone just to the south of the circle is the Northern Temperate Zone. The North Pole lies about 1,600 miles from the Arctic Circle.

There are seven countries that have significant territory within the Arctic Circle: Russia, Finland, Sweden, Norway, Canada, Greenland, and the United States (Alaska). While many mistakenly count Iceland as part of the Arctic Circle, the line only passes peripherally through one or two of this tiny nation's isles. However, most of Greenland lies inside the Arctic Circle.

FYI: There are 180,000 people living in Lapland and more than 200,000 reindeer.

Getting Around the Arctic

Norway, Sweden, and Finland have built railroads in the Arctic. Furthermore, Russia has two railroads that extend to Murmansk and the Ural Mountains. There is ferry service seasonally. Additionally, there are highways across the Arctic, including Yukon Highway 5. Klondike Highway, and James Dalton Highway.

Locals and tourists alike get around using many different modes of transportation, including snowmobiles, sleds, snowshoes, boats, buses, and vehicles.

The History of Santa Claus

Santa Claus (also known as Saint Nicholas, Father Christmas, and Kris Kringle) brings gifts to "good" boys and girls on Christmas. The modern concept of Santa Claus evolved from Saint Nicholas, who was a 4th century bishop and gift giver of Myra, the Dutch Sinterklaas, the British figure, Father Christmas, and the Germanic god Wodan and midwinter Yule.

An illustration appeared in *Harper's* magazine in 1866 declaring Santa's home as the North Pole. In 1927, Finnish broadcaster, Markus Rautio, claimed that Santa's workshop had been found in Ear Fell, Lapland. After that, it was universally accepted that Santa lived in Lapland. Santa later "moved" from the remote mountainous Korvtunturi region near Russia to the more-centrally located Rovaniemi.

Rovaniemi

During WWII, the city was bombed by the Russians, captured by the Nazis, and then devastated by retreating German troops. Reconstruction was made possible by UNICEF. Former First Lady Eleanor Roosevelt, who played a large role in UNICEF, visited Rovaniemi in 1950. An Arctic cabin was built in her honor. Her visit inspired the town to reinvent itself. Rovaniemi began promoting itself as a winter wonderland and the home of Santa. By the early 1980s, the province had been declared "Santa Claus Land." By 1985, Santa Claus

Village had opened and tourists from around the
world have come to enjoy this magical, fun
place.

Gifts for Santa

In the U.S. and Canada, children set out milk
and cookies for him (and carrots for the
reindeer) on Christmas Eve.

In the U.K. and Australia, mince pies and a beer are left out for him on Christmas Eve.

In Norway, Denmark, and Sweden, children set out porridge for Santa.

In Ireland, Christmas pudding and Guinness are left out for Santa.

In Chile, Pan de Pascua (Easter Bread), is left out for Santa by the kids. This is a sponge cake flavored with candied fruit, ginger, and honey.

In France, kids leave biscuits out for Santa (Père Noël).

In Germany, children write letters to Santa. Sorry, no cookies, pudding, or biscuits!

In some cultures, such as in Argentina, nothing is left for Santa. Instead, hay, water, and carrots are left out for his animals.

Suggested Reading

Here are some excellent, academic references if you'd like to learn more about the Arctic region.

Bramwell, Martyn. 1998. *Polar Exploration: Journeys to the Arctic and Antarctic.* DK Discoveries Publishing, Inc., New York.

Crane, K., Galasso, J.L. 1999. *Arctic Environmental Atlas.* Office of Naval Research. Naval Research Laboratory. Hunter College.

Holland, Clive. 1994. *Farthest North: A History of North Polar Exploration in Eye-Witness Accounts.* Carroll & Graf Publishers, Inc., New York.

ANNUAL EVENTS & AVERAGE TEMPS

- **Kiruna Snow Festival** (January) celebrates the winter, the snow, and the return of light to the region. It takes includes many attractions for all ages, including snow sculptures and rock music.
- **The Arctic Comics Festival** (May) is open to comedians from all Nordic countries. The event includes not only comedy but also comedy- related cinema, dance, music and theatre.
- **Sodankyla Midnight Sun Film Festival** (June), in the Lappish town of Sodankyla, attracts thousands of moviegoers with its around the clock movies shown in multiple venues.
- **Jutajaiset International Folk Festival** (June) is about storytelling, music, and dance.
- **SimeRock** (July) An annual rock festival held in Rovaniemi.

- **Savonlinna Opera Festival** (July) hosted in the fifteenth century medieval Olavinlinna Castle, which is the world's northernmost medieval stone fortress The festival has been held in this historic castle since 1912.
- **Soroya Deep Sea Fishing Festival** (July) is open to all anglers with boats.
- **Pyha Unplugged** (August). This acoustic festival of music challenges well known Finnish rockers to entertain without any kind of special effects or amplification.

Public holidays:

January
1st New Year's Day
6th Epiphany

March
Good Friday

April
Easter Sunday
2nd Easter Monday

May
1st Labor Day
Ascension Day
Pentecost

June
Midsummer

November
All Saints' Day

December
6th Independence Day
25th Christmas Day
26th Boxing Day

Note: Some shops and banks may be closed on
holidays.

Average Temps

Here is a chart of temperature averages.

Be sure to pay attention to my packing list and
remember that you can rent or buy clothing/gear
in Lapland.

Most tour companies provide clothing/gear for a
specific excursion.

	Jan	Feb	Mar	Apr	May	Jun	Jul	Aug	Sep	Oct	Nov	Dec
°C	-9	-10	-6	2	9	14	17	15	10	4	-2	-6
°F	16	14	21	36	48	57	63	59	50	39	28	21

July is the hottest month in the Arctic with an
average of 14°C or 57°F. January is the coldest
month with an average of -15°C or 5°F.

FYI: In Finland gratuity is always included in the bill therefore tipping is not required. This applies to everything: restaurants, taxis, cafés, room service and more.

However, if you do feel that you have received great service, locals will gladly accept it.

Value Added Tax (VAT) in Finland is 24% or a bit less on certain items. A refund of the local VAT is available to visitors

For more information about VAT, https://ec.europa.eu/taxation_customs/individuals/travelling/travellers-leaving-eu/guide-vat-refund-visitors-eu_en

 ## What to Pack

Be sure to bring a waterproof camera or recorder if you want to take photos or video. At the very least, pack electronic equipment in a waterproof bag. You should keep your important documents, such as tickets, money, and passports, in a waterproof bag. Bring extra batteries, memory sticks/cards, a small flashlight, and chargers.

If you're going to be camping or renting a property, make sure to find out if you need to bring or rent towels, sleeping bags, linen, etc.

I carry large plastic zip top bags so I can store wet bathing suits or dirty shoes. Also, I can safely store snacks and my important documents in these clear, plastic bags so I can easily find what I need in a hurry.

If you wear glasses, bring a spare pair. If you take medication, bring enough to last three or four days longer than your trip, in case you get delayed.

If you are traveling with small children, be sure to check with your outfitter about clothing/gear. They typically do not have clothing/gear for children under the age of five, so you will have to bring everything you need or make sure you can rent or buy what you need upon arrival.

Winter:

- Thick wool socks

- Thermal underwear

- Wool sweater or heavy sweatshirt

- Dressy sweater or dress

- Waterproof Ski pants

- Fleece pants

- Wool or fleece gloves (you will be given heavy gloves to wear for snowmobiling, etc. but a good pair of gloves underneath will help keep your fingers from feeling the cold)

- Wool scarf and hat

- Snood (optional)

- Small waterproof backpack

- Bathing suit, sandals/flip flops, cover-up (for sauna/swimming, etc.)

- Ski/snow boots

- Hand warmer heat pack or hot water bottle

- SPF lip balm

- Lap blanket (optional as they are usually provided on sleigh rides, etc.)

FYI: Don't pack cotton clothing. Cotton absorbs moisture and quickly becomes a fabric that makes you colder rather than warmer.

Summer:

- Thermal underwear

- Wool sweater or sweatshirt

- Fleece pants

- Windproof/waterproof jacket

- Good hiking boots (insulated and waterproof)

- Sun glasses & UV sunblock

- Small waterproof backpack

- Insect repellent

- Bathing suit, sandals/flip flops, cover-up (for sauna/swimming, etc.)

*Don't forget to pack underwear, pajamas, medications, toiletries, and other essentials. You may want to pack a pair of sneakers for the plane/airport, lodge, Helsinki, etc.

**FYI: The best thing you can put on your
hands is Gore-Tex gloves or mittens (with
glove liners or thin gloves underneath). Gore-
Tex is one of the warmest, most waterproof
fabrics you can find. I wear Gore-Tex
clothing when I go whitewater rafting in very
cold rivers. Gloves allow for more flexibility
but mittens will keep your hands warmer.**

**Be sure to buy the right socks too.
Your feet and hands are the most vulnerable
when you are out for prolonged periods of
time, so you must protect them with the right
clothing/gear.**

TERRANCE ZEPKE
Series Reading Order
& Guide

Series List

Most Haunted Series
Terrance Talks Travel Series
Spookiest Series
Stop Talking Series
Carolinas for Kids Series
Ghosts of the Carolinas Series
Books & Guides for the Carolinas Series
Cheap Travel Series
& More Books by Terrance Zepke

≈

Introduction

Here is a list of titles by Terrance Zepke. They are presented in chronological order although they do not need to be read in any particular order.

Also included is an author bio, a personal message from Terrance, and some other information you may find helpful.

All books are available as eBooks and print books. They can be found on Amazon, Barnes and Noble, Kobo, Apple iBooks, Smashwords, or through your favorite independent bookseller.

You can also connect with Terrance on Twitter **@terrancezepke** or on

www.facebook.com/terrancezepke
www.pinterest.com/terrancezepke

Sign up to be the first to learn about new episodes of her travel show, travel tips, and free downloadable TRAVEL REPORTS, at www.terrancetalkstravel.com.

You can follow her travel show, **TERRANCE TALKS TRAVEL: ÜBER ADVENTURES on** www.blogtalkradio.com/terrancetalkstravel or subscribe to it at **iTunes.**

Warning: Listening to this show could lead to a spectacular South African safari, hot-air ballooning over the Swiss Alps, Disney Adventures, and Tornado Tours!

AUTHOR BIO

Terrance Zepke studied Journalism at the University of Tennessee and later received a Master's degree in Mass Communications from the University of South Carolina. She studied parapsychology at the renowned Rhine Research Center.

Zepke spends much of her time happily traveling around the world but always returns home to the Carolinas where she lives part-time in both states. She has written hundreds of articles and close to three dozen books. She is the host of *Terrance Talks Travel: Über Adventures* and co-host of *A Writer's Journey: From Blank Page to Published.* Additionally, this award-winning and best-selling author has been featured in many publications and programs, such as NPR, CNN, The Washington Post, Associated Press, Travel with Rick Steves, Around the World, Publishers Weekly, World Travel & Dining with Pierre Wolfe, Good Morning Show, The Learning Channel, and The Travel Channel.

When she's not investigating haunted places, searching for pirate treasure, or climbing lighthouses, she is most likely packing for her next adventure to some far flung place, such as Reykjavik or Kwazulu Natal. Some of her favorite adventures include piranha fishing on the Amazon, shark cage diving in South Africa, hiking the Andes Mountains Inca Trail, camping in the Himalayas, dog-sledding in the Arctic Circle, and a gorilla safari in the Congo.

≈

MOST HAUNTED SERIES

*A Ghost Hunter's Guide to the Most Haunted Places in
America* (2012)
*A Ghost Hunter's Guide to the Most Haunted Houses in
America* (2013)
*A Ghost Hunter's Guide to the Most Haunted Hotels &
Inns in America* (2014)
*A Ghost Hunter's Guide to the Most Haunted Historic
Sites in America* (2016)
*A Ghost Hunter's Guide to the Most Haunted Places in
the World* (2018)

*The Ghost Hunter's MOST HAUNTED Box Set (3 in 1):
Discover America's Most Haunted Destinations* (2016)

MOST HAUNTED and SPOOKIEST Sampler Box Set:
Featuring *A GHOST HUNTER'S GUIDE TO THE MOST
HAUNTED PLACES IN AMERICA* and *SPOOKIEST
CEMETERIES* (2017)

TERRANCE TALKS TRAVEL SERIES

Terrance Talks Travel: A Pocket Guide to South Africa (2015)

Terrance Talks Travel: A Pocket Guide to African Safaris (2015)

Terrance Talks Travel: A Pocket Guide to Adventure Travel (2015)

Terrance Talks Travel: A Pocket Guide to Florida Keys (including Key West & The Everglades) (2016)

Terrance Talks Travel: The Quirky Tourist Guide to Key West (2017)

Terrance Talks Travel: The Quirky Tourist Guide to Cape Town (2017)

Terrance Talks Travel: The Quirky Tourist Guide to Reykjavik (2017)

Terrance Talks Travel: The Quirky Tourist Guide to Charleston (2017)

Terrance Talks Travel: The Quirky Tourist Guide to Ushuaia (2017)

The Quirky Tourist Guide to Lapland (Arctic Circle) & Helsinki, Finland | Terrance Zepke

Terrance Talks Travel: The Quirky Tourist Guide to Antarctica (2017)

Terrance Talks Travel: The Quirky Tourist Guide to Machu Picchu & Cuzco (2017)

African Safari Box Set: Featuring TERRANCE TALKS TRAVEL: *A Pocket Guide to South Africa* and *TERRANCE TALKS TRAVEL: A Pocket Guide to African Safaris* (2017)

Terrance Talks Travel: CHEAP LONDON! (2017)

Terrance Talks Travel: CHEAP DISNEY! (2017)

Terrance Talks Travel: A Pocket Guide to Uganda & Rwanda (2018)

Terrance Talks Travel: The Quirky Tourist Guide to Kathmandu (Nepal) (2018)

Terrance Talks Travel: The Quirky Tourist Guide to Marrakesh (2018)

Terrance Talks Travel: The Quirky Tourist Guide to Edinburgh (2018)

Terrance Talks Travel: The Quirky Tourist Guide to the Arctic Circle (2018)

≈

SPOOKIEST SERIES

Spookiest Lighthouses (2013)
Spookiest Battlefields (2015)
Spookiest Cemeteries (2016)
Spookiest Objects (2017)
Spookiest Military Bases (2019)

Spookiest Box Set (3 in 1): Discover America's Most Haunted Destinations (2016)

≈

STOP TALKING SERIES

Stop Talking & Start Writing Your Book (2015)
Stop Talking & Start Publishing Your Book (2015)
Stop Talking & Start Selling Your Book (2015)

Stop Talking & Start Writing Your Book Series (3 in 1) Box Set (2016)

≈

CHEAP TRAVEL SERIES

How to Cruise Cheap! (2017)

How to Fly Cheap! (2017)

How to Travel Cheap! (2017)

How to Travel FREE or Get Paid to Travel! (2017)

CHEAP TRAVEL BOX SET: How to Cruise Cheap, How to Fly Cheap, How to Travel Cheap, and How to Travel FREE or Get Paid to Travel (2017)

≈

Message from the Author

The primary purpose of this guide is to introduce you to some titles you may not have known about. Another reason for it is to let you know all the ways you can connect with me. Authors love to hear from readers. We truly appreciate you more than you'll ever know. Please feel free to send me a comment or question via the comment form found on every page on www.terrancezepke.com and www.terrancetalkstravel.com or follow me on your favorite social media. Don't forget that you can also listen to my travel show, **Terrance Talks Travel: Über Adventures** on Blog Talk Radio and iTunes. The best way to make sure you don't miss any episodes of these shows (and find a complete archive of shows), new book releases and giveaways, contests, my TRIP PICK OF THE WEEK, cheap travel tips, free downloadable travel reports, and more is to subscribe to *Terrance Talks Travel* on www.terrancetalkstravel.com or *Mostly Ghostly* on www.terrancezepke.com.

Thank you for your interest and HAPPY READING!

Terrance

ABOUT HELSINKI

Helsinki Malmi Airport,
https://www.finavia.fi/en/airports/helsinki-airport

**It is a 60 – 80-minute flight from Helsinki to
Rovaniemi. There are several flights daily.**

Sightseeing Tips…

Enjoy a free walking tour with **Happy Guide Helsinki**. http://www.happyguidehelsinki.com/

Many of the top museums in Helsinki offer **free day**(s) every month, usually on Fridays.

Skywheel Helsinki offers 29 gondolas that provide a 360° view of the heart of Helsinki, its surroundings, cultural attractions and historical buildings. Admission is reduced with a Helsinki Card.

Buy a **Helsinki Card**. The card gives you unlimited public transport for 24-72 hours and free admission to more than 50 attractions. https://www.helsinkicard.com/helsinki-attractions/

Take a **Helsinki Sightseeing Canal Cruise**. This 90-minute scenic cruise shows you many great sights, including Suomenlinna and other islands. https://www.helsinkicard.com/helsinki-attractions/beautiful-canal-route.html

Take a 20-minute **vintage tram ride tour** departing from Market Square.

Enjoy a drink and a snack in the Clarion Hotel's **Sky Lounge and Bar**. The Nordic chic hotel is one of the city's tallest buildings, so the view is spectacular, especially at sunset.

Click on this link to find **accommodations**, ranging from camping to luxury hotels, http://www.discoveringfinland.com/metropolitan-area/helsinki/accommodation/.

Click on this link to see reviews for best **food and nightlife** in Helsinki, https://www.yelp.com/c/helsinki/nightlife.

Start your orientation tour with a **Hop-On, Hop-Off Helsinki Sightseeing Bus Tour**. Depending on the weather and your preference, you can sit inside the bus or the top is open. There are fifteen different stops and you can get on and off as often as you like during the 24-hours your ticket is valid. There is an audio tour that shares interesting facts about the city and sights. https://www.helsinkicard.com/helsinki-attractions/helsinki-hop-on-hop-off-bus-tour.html

If you're a born shopper, **Aleksanterinkatu Street** is one of the famous shopping streets in the city.

There are so many things to see and do in Helsinki that you should allow at least 2-3 days, if possible.

Here is a list and you can do what most interests you and/or what time permits:

____**Ateneum** (Finnish National Museum of Art); designed by Theodor Höijer and completed in 1887, the Ateneum holds Finland's finest art collection of historic works as well as a contemporary art gallery.

___**Central Library Oodi**; built in 2018 as a library and also includes a cinema, café, studios, special events center, and restaurant.

___**Central Park** (Keskuspuisto); located in the middle of the city and full of walking and biking trails.

___**Finnish National Gallery**

___**Gallen-Kallela Museum** showcases one of the most influential and important artists in Finland, Akseli Gallen-Kallela. The museum also has a gift shop and café.

___**Helsinki Art Museum** (HAM)

___**Hietaniemi** is a public beach, park, and cemetery.

___**Kamppi Chapel of Silence** (Finnish Lutheran Church)

___**Kiama** (Museum of Contemporary Art)

MY  *FAVORITE ATTRACTION...*

___**Korkeasaari Zoo** (Helsinki Zoo) is one of the oldest in the world dating back to the 1800s. It is renowned for its breeding programs for endangered species, especially with Siberian Tigers and Himalayan Snow Leopards. The zoo boasts more than 150 different species of animals and exotic tropical houses with 1,000 plant species. The natural habitat zoo is open year-round and is accessible by ferry from May-September and by bus the rest of the year. https://www.korkeasaari.fi/helsinki-zoo/

___**Linnanmaki Amusement Park** dates back to 1950; shops, rides (many roller coasters, a huge ferris wheel, river rafting, and water rides), shows, and lots of food vendors. Summer only.

___**Market Square (Kauppatori)**); great shopping & food.

___**Malminkartanonhuippu** is an artificial hill with a height of 90 meters above sea level. It is the highest point in the city with a 360° panorama view in all directions. You only have to climb 426 steps to get to the view!

___**Military Museum of Finland**

___**National Museum of Finland** (Kansallismuseo); features costumes and cultural objects of Finland.

___**Natural History Museum of Helsinki**, dating back to 1924, has botanical, zoological, biological, and geological collections.

___**Parliament House** (pictured here)

___**Senate Square;** the square is dominated by four buildings, including Helsinki Cathedral (most photographed building in Finland), Government Palace, the main building of the University of Helsinki, and the National Library of Finland. A statue of Alexander II stands in the middle of the square.

___**Serena** is the largest waterpark in Finland and is suitable for small children. Part of the park is open year round and all of the park during the summer.

Helsinki Cathedral

___**Seurasaari;** open-air museum with old
houses, farmsteads, a manor house, a church
from Kiruna (1686), and other timber buildings
that have been brought here for all parts of
Finland.

___**Sibelius Monument and Park**

Sibelius Monument plays music when the wind blows through it.

___Suomenlinna & Sveaborg Castle; UNESCO World Heritage Site accessible by 20-minute ferry ride

___Temppeliaukio Church (Rock Church); underground interior of the church was carved out of and built directly into the ancient solid rock of the Helsinki peninsula.

____ **Uspensky Russian Orthodox Cathedral**
features towers, spires, and gold cupolas. Its
interior is full of marble and gold
embellishments.

FYI: My favorite building in Helsinki is the Pohjola Insurance Building. See if you can find all the gnomes, witches, and animals carved into it!

**FYI: The Helsinki Olympic Stadium
includes a Swimming Stadium that is open to
the public during the summer.**

Day Trips: Ainola, Hameenlinna, Hanko,
Hvittrask, Pihlajasaari, Porvoo, and Tapiola.

Tallinn, Estonia (pictured here) is an easy day
trip by ferry. I loved its cobblestone streets and
historic squares. It is a medieval city (Old Town)
that has an intriguing history and lots of nice
shops and eateries.

Just For Fun…

- There are more women than men in Helsinki (55% women vs. 45% men).

- There are eight public saunas in Helsinki.

- Helsinki enjoys 18+ hours of daylight during summers. During winters, the nights are longer with 18+ hours of darkness.

- Popular souvenirs include salty canned/dried reindeer meat, jam, salty licorice, Moomins, and Finnish glassware.

- It is estimated that each Finn drinks about twenty-nine pounds of coffee per year. The oldest coffee café in Helsinki is Ekberg (1852).

- Be sure to wear good walking shoes. Helsinki has 80+ museums and galleries.

- There are six universities in Helsinki.

- Finland has more forests than any other country in Europe with 86% of its land covered in forest area.

  - Take a Murder Walk where you'll learn about some of the most shocking crimes in Helsinki history.

http://www.discoveringfinland.com/destin
ation/murder-walk-r-13/

- Helsinki is the world's coldest capital,
  with a yearly average temperature not
  exceeding 0°C, but there is no snow on
  the sidewalks and boulevards of central
  Helsinki during the winter. The city heats
  the granite slabs from underground, so
  precipitation melts immediately.

- They have odd annual events, including
  wife carrying, mobile phone throwing,
  and four public restaurant days, meaning
  that during these specific days anyone can
  open a pop up restaurant without a license
  or permit.

Short History of Helsinki

Helsinki is the largest city in Finland and its capital. Helsinki has a population of 629,512, an urban population of 1,214,210, and a metropolitan population of over 1.4 million .It was founded in the Middle Ages to be a rival to other ports on the Gulf of Finland, but it remained a small fishing village for over two centuries. Its importance grew increased when Sveaborg was constructed at the entrance to the harbor. Despite the fortress, Helsinki was forced to surrender to Russia during the Finnish War, and Finland was assimilated into the Russian Empire as part of the 'Treaty of Fredrikshamn'. Russia moved the Finnish capital from Turku to Helsinki. The city grew at a rapid pace during the 19th century. Helsinki is close in proximity (and has close ties) to three key European cities: Tallinn, Estonia; Stockholm, Sweden; and St. Petersburg, Russia. Helsinki is Finland's epicenter for politics, education, finance, culture, and research.

INDEX

U

Uspensky Russian Orthodox Cathedral, 137

V

Made in the USA
Monee, IL
19 May 2022